T0040685

A SECOND LATIN-AMERICAN FLUTE ALBUM

EDITED BY TREVOR WYE

for flute and piano

NOVELLO PUBLISHING LIMITED

Order No: NOV120635

While every effort has been made to trace all owners of
copyright material included in this collection, any omission is
regretted and should be brought to the attention of the publisher.

© Copyright 1987 Novello & Company Limited
All Rights Reserved

No part of this publication may be copied or reproduced in any form or by any means without
the prior permission of Novello & Company Limited.

CONTENTS

PREFACE

A fascination of many years standing for the rhythms and melodies of South American music has resulted in the compiling of these volumes. The rhythms, for those of us from other countries are, at first, difficult but with a little practice, they will become easier. Those pieces in five beats in a bar are best practised at one beat in a bar. Where marked 8va, this is optional, though Latin-American flautists are noted for their ease in the top register.

Ornaments have been suggested; more can be added. A bass + percussion part can be added, if required. Syncopation, in this music, is impossible to write down accurately. The solution is to relax and enjoy this special rhythmic style.

I am indebted to Robert Scott for his immense patience in arranging the piano parts.

Trevor Wye

The separate flute part is inserted

A SECOND LATIN-AMERICAN FLUTE ALBUM

Edited by Trevor Wye

PASAJE NO. 1

(Passage No. 1)

S. Torrealba

* Percussion rhythm | ♫ 𝄾 ♫ ♫ | optional

© Copyright 1987 Novello & Company Limited

All Rights Reserved

2. SOL EN MERENGUE
(Merengue sun)

Folk

10

3. EL FRUTERO

(The Greengrocer)

Folk

A SECOND LATIN-AMERICAN FLUTE ALBUM

EDITED BY TREVOR WYE

for flute and piano

FLUTE

NOVELLO PUBLISHING LIMITED

Order No: NOV120635

4. BAILECITO DE PROCESION
(Little Dance Procession)

Folk Tune
adapted by Gustavo Samela

© 1972 by Ricordi Americana S.A.E.C., Cangallo 1558, Buenos Aires, Argentina.
Unique edition authorized by Ricordi Americana S.A.E.C. of Buenos Aires, Argentina, owner of world-wide rights.

5. EL CAMALEON
(The Chameleon)

Folk

6. EL QUINTAPESARES
(The Consolation)

Folk

Music for Flute

Solo

Gordon Saunders
Eight Traditional Japanese Pieces
Gordon Saunders has selected and transcribed these pieces for tenor recorder solo or flute from the traditional folk music of Japan.

Trevor Wye
Practice Book for the Flute

Volume 1	TONE
Volume 2	TECHNIQUE
Volume 3	ARTICULATION
Volume 4	INTONATION
Volume 5	BREATHING AND SCALES
Volume 6	ADVANCED PRACTICE

Flute & Piano

Richard Rodney Bennett
Summer Music *Associated Board Grade VII*

Charles Camilleri
Sonata Antica

François Couperin
A Couperin Album *arranged by Trevor Wye*

James Galway
Showpieces
The Magic Flute of James Galway
Two albums, each containing ten favourite pieces by various composers, arranged for flute and piano by James Galway. Both include photographs and a separate flute part.

Michael Hurd
Sonatina

John McCabe
Portraits *Associated Board Grades V & VI*

Jean Philippe Rameau
A Rameau Album *arranged by Trevor Wye*

Eric Satie
A Satie Flute Album *arranged by Trevor Wye*

Gerard Schurmann
Sonatina

Antonio Vivaldi
A Vivaldi Album *arranged by Trevor Wye*